31 Paleo

A Month Long Paleo Fiesta

MARY SCOTT

DISCLAIMER

varies and could result in the need for longer or shorter cooking times. All precautions should be taken to ensure food is fully cooked in order to prevent risk of foodborne illnesses. The author and publisher do not take responsibility for any consequences that are believed to be a result of following the instructions in this book.

INTRODUCTION

There is something about the distinct combination of Mexican flavors that make Mexican dishes sing and diners want to dance. The spicy, savory and tangy ingredients create a fine medley for any palate, and result in delicious, hearty meals and appetizers that are always party favorites. And now with 31 Days of Paleo Mexican you can enjoy those superb dishes while sticking to your clean eating Paleo plan.

It may seem Paleo and Mexican food are incongruous, however for the 31 Days of Paleo Mexican we have created a list of recipes that completely harmonize the two. Check out Paleo Nachos made with Sweet Potato Chips, Pepper Steak Fajitas and the fantastic Pork Carnitas. These dishes will make you forget that we've tweaked the recipes to move in line with Paleo dietary requirements that do not allow for Dairy and Grains.

The recipes in the 31 Days of Paleo Mexican use great subs for standard Mexican recipes that allow you to enjoy the softness of fajitas and the crunchiness of chips without using traditional grains. In addition we have created a section entitled Bases, in this section you get recipes for Paleo Sour Cream, Salsa, and Guacamole, some of the standard items you're going to want to have around when whipping up your Mexican Fiesta.

This book will get you through football get-togethers, Halloween parties and help you whip up delicious family meals. The ingredients are clean and healthy while the flavors pack a punch. Enjoy these recipes throughout the year and maybe enjoy create a special Paleo Fiesta party of your own.

Here's to Paleo gone deliciously Mexican!

Table of Contents

APPETIZERS

Pork Carnitas on Roast Pepper Bites
Serves: 24
Prep Time: 30 Minutes

Ingredients

2 lbs. pork shoulder, boneless
1/2 cup orange juice
1/2 cup low-sodium chicken stock
12 small sweet peppers,
2 tsps. Cumin, oregano
1 tsp. paprika
3 tsp. salt, black pepper
2 tbsp. coconut oil

Directions

Coat pork shoulder with coconut oil and rub in spices and salt.

Place pork shoulder in 4 qt. Slow cooker, add orange juice and cook on low for 8 hours in sauce.

Preheat oven to 400 degrees, place parchment on roasting pan.

Chop sweet peppers in half, place on roasting pan, spoon Carnitas into peppers, roast in oven for 15 minutes.

Nutrition (g)
Calories 135
Fat 9
Sodium 321
Carbs 3
Protein 9

The Ultimate Paleo 7-Layer Mexican Dip
Serves: 6
Prep Time: 25 minutes

Ingredients

Layer 1
1 lb. lean ground beef
1 white onion, peeled, diced
6 cloves garlic, peeled, minced
3 tbsp. organic tomato paste
Coconut oil for cooking

Layer 2
2 red onions, peeled, diced

Layer 3
2 avocados, pitted, peeled
1 lime, juiced
1/2 tsp. salt

Layer 4
1 cup almonds, soaked overnight, peeled

Layer 5
1 cup Paleo salsa

Layer 6
2 cups romaine lettuce, chopped

Layer 7
1 cup Paleo sour cream

Directions

For Layer 1 place 2 tbsp. coconut oil in skillet over medium heat, add ground beef, garlic, onions and cook until beef is browned, add tomato paste and cook for another 3 minutes, set aside.

For Layer 3, quarter avocado, place in blender with lime juice and salt, blend until smooth.

In glass bowl, place beef layer on bottom and add remaining layers by number.

Serve with Beetroot or Sweet Potato chips

Nutrition (g)
Calories 370
Fat 22
Sodium 257 (mg)
Carbs 16
Protein 28

Mango Jalapeno Guacamole
Serves: 4
Prep Time: 15 Minutes

Ingredients

2 avocados, seeded, peeled
1 mango, pitted, peeled
1 jalapeno, seeded, minced
1 cup cilantro, chopped
2 limes, juiced
1 tsp. salt, black pepper

Directions

Rough chop avocado and mango.

Place avocado into food processor with lime juice and blend until smooth.

Add remaining ingredients and pulse until well combined.

Serve with Sweet Potato Nacho Chips (Recipe in Basics)

Nutrition (g)
Calories 137
Fat 13
Sodium 392
Carbs 6
Protein 1

Lime Zing Shrimp Ceviche
Serves: 4
Prep Time: 10 Minutes

Ingredients

1 lb. shrimp, cleaned
2 limes, juiced
1 serrano, seeded, minced
1 lemon, juiced
1 tomato, diced
1 small cucumber, diced
¼ cup tomato sauce
½ tsp. salt, black pepper

Directions

Combine ingredients in bowl, cover and refrigerate for an hour.

Nutrition (g)
Calories 163
Fat 2
Sodium 651 (mg)
Carbs 9
Protein 27

Bacon-Stuffed Jalapenos
Serves: 4-6
Prep Time: 20 Minutes

Ingredients

8 jalapenos
4 bacon strips, cooked, chopped
¾ cup cashews, soaked overnight
4 cloves garlic, minced
1 small onion, diced
½ tsp. oregano, cumin
½ tsp. salt, black pepper
Coconut oil for cooking

Directions

Preheat oven to 350 degrees and place sheet of parchment paper on baking sheet.

Slice jalapenos in half, remove seeds, set aside.

Heat 2 tbsp. coconut oil in skillet over medium.

Add onions, garlic and sauté for a minute.

Place garlic, onion, cashews, salt and spices in food processor.

Mix until smooth, using spoon, mix in bacon.

Lay jalapenos halves on baking sheet and spoon in cashew mixture.

Bake for 15 minutes.

Nutrition (g)
Calories 248
Fat 19
Sodium 556 (mg)
Carbs 13
Protein 10

Paleo Nachos
Serves: 4-6
Prep Time: 15 minutes

Ingredients

Meat Sauce
1 lb. lean ground beef
1 onion, diced
4 cloves garlic, minced
4 cups tomato puree
1 tsp. cumin, oregano
1 tsp. salt, black pepper

Topping
1 avocado, pitted, diced
1 onion, diced
2 tomatoes, diced
½ cup cilantro, chopped
1 lime, juiced
½ tsp. salt, black pepper

Base
4 servings Sweet Potato Chips (Recipe in Basics)

Directions

For the sauce heat 2 tbsp. ground beef in skillet, Add ground beef, sauté for two minutes, add garlic, onion.

Sauté ingredients until beef is browned, add salt, spices and tomato puree.

Cover, simmer for 10 minutes.

Toss ingredients for toppings together.

Plate sweet potato chips, top with meat sauce and avocado topping.

Nutrition (g) (meat sauce and topping)
Calories 450
Fat 18
Sodium 1025
Carbs 36
Protein 41

SOUPS AND SALADS

Soup of the Seven Seas
Serves: 8
Prep Time: 10 Minutes

Ingredients

1 lb. medium shrimp, shelled
1 lb. mussels, shelled
2-1/2 lbs. Tilapia fillets
1 onion, peeled, diced
4 cloves, garlic
4 dried Guajillo chilies
1 red bell pepper, diced
1 cup epazote, chopped (use cilantro if not available)
6 cups low-sodium chicken broth
1 lime, juiced
Coconut oil for cooking

Directions

Slice Tilapia into 2" pieces.

Heat 4 tbsp. coconut oil in Dutch oven over medium heat.

Add chilies, onions, bell pepper and sauté for 3-4 minutes.

Brown fish in Dutch oven, pour in blender sauce. Add remaining ingredients, cover, reduce heat to low and simmer for 20 minutes.

Nutrition (g)
Calories 231
Fat 4
Sodium 385
Carbs 6
Protein 42

Caldo de Pollo (Mexican Chicken Soup with Tortilla)
Serves: 4
Prep Time: 25 minutes

Ingredients

1/2 lb. chicken breast, skinless
1 lb. chicken legs/thighs, skinless
1/2 medium cabbage
1 sweet potato, peeled, cubed
1 onion, peeled, chopped
4 cloves, garlic, peeled, minced
3 carrots, peeled, sliced
2 cups tomato, pureed
2 cups low-sodium chicken stock
1/2 cup cilantro chopped
1/2 tsp. cumin, oregano
1 tsp. salt, black pepper
Coconut oil for cooking
2 Almond Tortillas (Recipe in Basics)

Directions

Separate cabbage leaves, chop into 3" wide pieces, set aside.

Cube chicken breast into 1" pieces

Heat 4 tbsp. coconut oil in Dutch oven.

Brown chicken breast, thighs, legs.

Remove from pan.

Add onions, carrots, sweet potato, and sauté for five minutes.

Return chicken to pan, add remaining ingredients, save cilantro, bring to boil.

Reduce heat and simmer on low for 45 minutes.

Slice almond tortillas into 2" triangles.

Pour enough coconut oil to cover the bottom of a small frying pan, brown tortilla chips.

Top soup with cilantro and tortilla chips.

Nutrition (g)
Calories 401
Fat 15
Sodium 792 (mg)
Carbs 16
Protein 50

Creamy Ancho Soup
Serves: 6
Prep Time: 10 Minutes

Ingredients

6 dried ancho chilies, seeded, stemmed
1 onion, peeled, diced
3 cloves garlic, peeled, minced
1 can coconut milk
3 cups low-sodium chicken stock
1 tsp. oregano, dried cumin
1/2 tsp. paprika
1 tsp. salt, black pepper
Coconut oil for cooking

Directions

Heat 3 tbsp. coconut oil in non-stock pot.

Add onion, garlic, chilies and sauté for 3 minutes.

Stir in chicken stock, spices, salt, bring to boil.

Reduce heat, cover and simmer for 15 minutes.

Using hand immersion blender, blend until smooth.

Mix in coconut cream and simmer on low for another 5 minutes.

Nutrition (g)
Calories 220
Fat 14
Sodium 692 (mg)
Carbs 7
Protein 3

Roasted Tomatillo Chicken Soup

Serves: 4
Prep Time: 10 Minutes

Ingredients

1-1/2 lb. chicken breast, skinless, boneless, cubed
1 red bell pepper, seeded, diced
4 tomatillos, husked, diced
1 Poblano Pepper
1 onion, peeled, diced
3 cloves garlic, minced
1 lime, juiced
1/2 cup cilantro, chopped.
2 cups low-sodium chicken stock
3 cups water
1 tsp. salt, black pepper

Directions

Preheat oven to 400 degrees, brush poblano pepper and tomatillos with a little coconut oil and place on roasting tray and into oven for 10 minutes.

Cool, remove poblano skin, chop, set poblano and tomatillos aside.

Place 3 tbsp. coconut oil in nonstick pot over medium heat.

Add chicken breasts, brown, remove.

Add onions, garlic, and sauté for 2 minutes until fragrant.

Add tomatillos, liquids, salt and pepper, cover, bring to boil.

Using hand immersion blender, blend until smooth. Stir in poblano pepper and chicken, cover and simmer on low for 20 minutes

Stir in cilantro in last five minutes.

Nutrition (g)
Calories 230
Fat 5
Sodium 788 (mg)
Carbs 8
Protein 38

Hearty Beef Chili
Serves: 6-8
Prep Time: 15 Minutes

Ingredients

2 lbs. stewing beef
2 onions, diced
6 cloves garlic, minced
1 tsp. chipotle paste
4 cups crushed tomatoes
2 cups low-sodium beef stock
1 tsp. cinnamon
1 tsp. cumin, oregano
1 tsp. salt, black pepper
Coconut oil for cooking

Directions

Lightly coat 4 qt. slow cooker with coconut oil.

Add ingredients, cook on low for 7 hours.

Nutrition (g)
Calories 373
Fat 10
Sodium 818 (mg)
Carbs 19
Protein 51

Chili Verde

Serves: 4
Prep Time: 20 Minutes

Ingredients

1 lb. boneless pork
1 tomatillo, husked, chopped
2 Poblano chilies
2 onions, diced
4 cloves garlic, minced
2 cups low-sodium chicken broth
1 tsp. oregano, cumin, paprika
2 tsp. salt, black pepper
Coconut oil for cooking

Directions

Preheat oven to 400 degrees, line baking sheet with parchment paper, place poblanos on sheet and roast for 10 Minutes
Peel poblanos and remove seeds, chop and sprinkle with ½ tsp. salt, set aside.
Slice pork into ½" cubes.
Heat 2 tbsp. coconut oil in skillet, add pork and brown.
Place pork, poblanos and remaining ingredients in 4 qt. slow-cooker and cook on high for 2 hours.

Nutrition (g)
Calories 258
Fat 8
Sodium 1262 (mg)
Carbs 7
Protein 37

Avocado Lime Salad
Serves: 4
Prep Time: 10 minutes

Ingredients

Salad
3 cups Romaine lettuce, chopped
2 red bell peppers, seeded, chopped
5 radishes, peeled, sliced
1 avocado, pitted, peeled, diced
2 tomatoes, diced

Orange-Lime Dressing
2 limes, juiced
1/4 cup orange juice
1/2 cup cilantro, chopped
1/4 cup coconut oil
1/2 tsp. salt, black pepper

Directions

Combine dressing ingredients and whisk. Toss salad ingredients in large bowl and combine with dressing just before serving.

Nutrition (g)
Calories 284
Fat 24
Sodium 16 (mg)
Carbs 13
Protein 3

Mexican Taco Salad
Serves: 4
Prep Time: 10 Minutes

Ingredients

2 cups romaine lettuce, chopped
1 lb. lean ground beef
1 tomato, diced
1 onion, peeled, diced
1 carrot, grated
1 avocado, pitted, sliced
1 cup almonds, soaked overnight
1 lemon, juiced
1 tsp. cumin, oregano
1 tsp. salt, black pepper
2 almond tortillas (Recipe in Basics)
Salsa (Recipe in Basics)
Paleo sour cream (Recipe in Basics)

Directions

Peel almonds, sprinkle with ½ tsp. cumin, oregano, salt, black pepper and mix in juice of one lemon and refrigerate for 10 Minutes

Combine lettuce, tomato, onion, carrot, and avocado, set aside.

In skillet heat 2 tbsp. coconut oil, add beef, salt, spices and brown, set aside.

Heat 2 tbsp. coconut oil in skillet over medium heat.

Lightly Fry almond tortillas until browned.

Place tortilla in bowl, scoop in salad, top with almonds, salsa, Paleo sour cream.

Nutrition (g)
Calories 279
Fat 20
Sodium 377 (mg)
Carbs 8
Protein 22

MAIN DISHES

Rainbow Chicken Quesadilla
Serves: 6
Prep Time:

Ingredients

1 lb. chicken breast
1 each green, red, yellow bell peppers, seeded, sliced
2 onions, peeled, sliced
4 cloves garlic, peeled, minced
1 tsp. cumin, oregano, paprika
1 tsp. salt, black pepper
Coconut oil for cooking
6 almond tortillas (Recipe in Basics)
Salsa (Recipe in Basics)
Paleo sour cream (Recipe in Basics)

Directions

Slice chicken breast into 1" wide strips.

Heat 4 tbsp. coconut oil in skillet.

Sauté chicken for 4-5 minutes, until browned and cooked through.

Remove from skillet, set aside.

Add a little more coconut oil if needed.

Toss in onions, garlic, and sauté until onion is translucent.

Add green peppers and sauté for another 3 minutes.

Add chicken and spices, salt, pepper, mix on stove top for a few minutes.

Preheat oven to 375 degrees, lightly coat 6 x 9 glass baking dish with coconut oil.
Grab tortilla, place mixture on half of tortilla, top with a tbsp. of salsa, fold over and place in baking dish, repeat.

Bake in oven for 15 minutes.

Serve with salsa and paleo sour cream.

Nutrition (g) (filling)
Calories 273
Fat 9
Sodium 684 (mg)
Carbs 12
Protein 34

Pineapple Pork Tacos
Serves: 4
Prep Time: 15 minutes

Ingredients

1 lb. ground pork
1 medium onion, peeled, diced
1 tomato, diced
6 cloves garlic
½ cup fresh pineapple, diced
1 head Boston lettuce, washed
1 tsp. cumin, oregano
1/2 tsp. paprika
1 tsp. salt, black pepper
Coconut oil for cooking

Toppings
Salsa
Sour Cream

Directions

Heat 3 tbsp. coconut oil in skillet over medium, add garlic, onion and sauté until onion is translucent.

Add ground beef, brown.

Add pineapple, spices, salt, black pepper and sauté for two minutes.

Choose large pieces from heat of Boston lettuce.

27

Spoon beef onto lettuce shells and top with salsa and sour cream.

Nutrition (g)
Calories 208
Fat 4
Sodium 657
Carbs 10
Protein 31

Chunky Avocado Burrito
Serves: 4
Prep Time: 20 Minutes

Ingredients

1 lb. lean ground beef
2 medium onions, diced
1 avocado, peeled, pitted, diced
6 cloves garlic, minced
2 jalapenos
2 limes, juiced
1 tsp. cumin, oregano
1 tsp. black pepper, salt
Coconut oil for cooking
8 almond tortillas
Paleo refried beans

Directions

Place 2 tbsp. coconut oil in skillet over medium heat, add onion, garlic, jalapeno, sauté for a minute, remove half mixture and place in bowl.

Add beef, brown, add spices, and mix well.

In a bowl, combine chunky avocado with lime juice and jalapeno onion mixture.

Place almond tortilla on plate, spoon in beef mixture, and top with chunky avocado and Paleo refried beans, wrap up into burrito and repeat.

Nutrition (g)
Calories 347
Fat 17
Sodium 80 (mg)
Carbs 12
Protein 36

Chipotle Bacon Chicken
Serves: 4
Prep Time: 10 Minutes

Ingredients

4 4 oz. chicken breasts
4 slices bacon, cooked
2 chipotle peppers, sliced
2 tbsp. tomato paste
4 cloves garlic, minced
1 tsp. salt, black pepper, cumin
Coconut oil for cooking

Directions

Preheat oven to 400 degrees, line baking dish with parchment.

Place chipotle peppers, garlic, tomato paste, salt, pepper, cumin in food processor and mix until paste. Slice bacon into little strips and mix into chipotle paste.

Coat chicken with paste, place on parchment and bake in oven for 25 minutes, turning halfway.

Nutrition (g)
Calories 358
Fat 19
Sodium 1128 (mg)
Carbs 5

Protein 41

Pepper Steak Fajitas
Serves: 4
Prep Time: 15 Minutes

Ingredients

1 lb. strip steak
1/2 cauliflower head
1 onion, peeled, diced
4 cloves garlic, peeled, minced
1 cup low-sodium chicken broth
1/2 tsp. cumin, oregano
1 tsp. salt
2 tbsp. coarse black pepper
6 almond tortillas
Coconut oil for cooking

Toppings
Salsa
Guacamole

Directions

Rub steak with black pepper and slice against the grain into 1/2" wide strips, set aside.

Chop cauliflower florets into rice-like granules, set aside.

Heat 2 tbsp. coconut oil in skillet, add onions, garlic and sauté for two minutes.

Add cauliflower, sauté for 3 minutes.

Add chicken stock, reduce heat to low, cover and cook for 10 minutes.

In a separate skillet, heat 3 tbsp. coconut oil over medium, add steak and sauté until browned, sprinkle with a little cumin and oregano.

Spoon steak into almond tortillas, top with cauliflower rice, salsa, guacamole.

Nutrition (g)
Calories 144
Fat 2
Sodium 978 (mg)
Carbs 9
Protein 24

Mexican Lime Shrimp Lettuce Wraps
Serves: 4
Prep Time:

Ingredients

1 lb. shrimp, cooked
1 head Boston lettuce
2 limes, juiced
1 scallion, minced
½ tsp. cumin, oregano, paprika
1 tsp. salt, black pepper
½ cup salsa

Directions

Combine shrimp with lime, spices, salt and scallion, refrigerate for half an hour.

Spoon lime shrimp on one lettuce leaf, top with salsa.

Nutrition (g)
Calories 148
Fat 2
Sodium 867 (mg)
Carbs 5
Protein 27

Chicken Tostadas
Serves: 4
Prep Time: 15 Minutes

Ingredients

3 cups cooked chicken breast
2 limes, juiced
1/2 tsp. salt, black pepper
Coconut oil for cooking
6 Cauliflower Tortillas
Paleo refried beans, mashed

Topping
Salsa
Sour cream
Handful cilantro, chopped

Directions

Combine chicken breast with lime juice and 1/2 tsp. salt and 1/2 tsp. black pepper, marinate for an hour. Heat 1/4 cup coconut oil in medium skillet, cook each cauliflower tortilla for about three minutes to get a crunch.

Spread tortilla with mashed Paleo Refried Beans mixture and top with lime chicken.

Next add lettuce, salsa, sour cream and a sprinkling of cilantro.

Nutrition (g) (filling)
Calories 185
Fat 4
Sodium 420 (mg)
Carbs 0
Protein 36

Beef Baracoa
Serves: 8
Prep Time:

Ingredients

2 lbs. Beef chuck roast
1 medium onion, peeled, sliced
1 medium tomato, diced
10 cloves garlic, peeled, chopped
6 dried guajillo chilies
1 tsp. cumin, oregano
1/2 tsp. cinnamon, paprika, thyme
1 cup cilantro, chopped
1 lime, juiced
2 tsp. salt
2 tbsp. coarse black pepper
2 bay leaves
Coconut oil for cooking
6 cauliflower tortillas
Guacamole
Paleo Sour Cream

Directions

Heat 3 tbsp. coconut oil in Dutch oven over medium.

Add garlic, onions, sauté until onion is translucent.

Add tomato and chilies and cook for five minutes
allowing moisture to evaporate.

37

Pour ingredients into blender and mix until smooth.

Cut beef into 1" cubes. Add to skillet and brown.

Add chili sauce back to skillet along with cilantro, spices and salt.

Cover, reduce heat to low, simmer for 2-1/2 hours. Remove bay leaves, use fork to shred roast, and serve on Cauliflower tortillas with Guacamole and Paleo Sour Cream.

Nutrition (g)
Calories 353
Fat 13
Sodium 880 (mg)
Carbs 6
Protein 51

Delicious Paleo Pork Posole
Serves: 8-10
Prep Time: 15 Minutes

Ingredients

3 lbs. pork butt
1 medium onion, diced
3 cups butternut squash
5 cloves garlic, minced
2 tomatoes, diced
2 cups low-sodium chicken stock
½ cup cilantro, chopped
2 tsp. oregano, cumin, black pepper
1 tbsp. salt
Coconut oil for cooking

Directions

Lightly coat 4 qt. slow cooker with coconut oil.

Rub pork butt with salt and spices, place in slow cooker.

Add remaining ingredients.

Cook on low for eight hours.

Remove pork butt from slow cooker, shred with fork, return to posole and sprinkle dish with cilantro.

Nutrition (g)
Calories 369
Fat 12
Sodium 1006 (mg)
Carbs 10
Protein 54

BASICS

Cauliflower Tortillas
Serves: 4
Prep Time: 15 Minutes

Ingredients

5 cups grated, cauliflower
2 eggs
1/2 tsp. salt, black pepper
1 tsp. coconut oil

Directions

Preheat oven to 375 degrees.

Squeeze grated cauliflower to remove as much fluid as possible.

Whisk eggs, add to cauliflower along with coconut oil, salt and pepper.

Lay down sheets of parchment paper to fit 6" tortillas. Drop tortilla mixture onto parchment and shape into 6" tortillas.

Place another parchment sheet on top of each tortilla.

Place in oven for 10 minutes, turning halfway.

To get a little crunch, heat skillet and toast tortillas for a minute each side.

Nutrition (g)
Calories 72
Fat 3
Sodium 359 (mg)
Carbs 7
Protein 5

Almond Tortillas
Serves: 8
Prep Time: 15 Minutes

Ingredients

2 ½ cups almond flour
½ tsp. salt
1 small egg
2 tbsp. water
½ tsp. agave nectar
Coconut oil

Directions
Whisk egg, combine with flour, salt, agave nectar and 1 tsp. coconut oil.

Knead into dough, separate into 8 balls

Place wax paper on flat surface, grab one ball, place on wax paper, take a second piece of wax paper and place over ball.

Roll into tortilla.

Heat 2 tbsp. coconut oil in skillet, place tortilla in skillet and cook 3 minutes per side.

Nutrition (g)
Calories 222
Fat 21
Sodium 166 (mg)
Carbs 9
Protein 4

Paleo Sour Cream
Serves: 6
Prep Time: 10 Minutes

Ingredients

1 cup coconut cream
3 tbsp. fresh lemon juice
1/2 tsp. salt

Directions

Combine ingredients, refrigerate for an hour at least before serving.

Nutrition (g)
Calories 94
Fat 10
Sodium 201 (mg)
Carbs 2
Protein 1

Spicy Salsa
Serves: 6
Prep Time: 10 Minutes

Ingredients

2 green bell peppers, seeded, diced
2 red bell peppers, seeded, diced
1 onion, peeled, sliced
6 cloves garlic, peeled, minced
2 cups crushed tomatoes
1/2 cup balsamic vinegar
1 tsp. cumin, oregano
1/2 tsp. paprika
1 tsp. cayenne pepper
1 tsp. salt, cracked black pepper

Directions

Mix ingredients in bowl, refrigerate for 2 hours before serving.

Nutrition (g)
Calories 76
Fat 0
Sodium 553 (mg)
Carbs 15
Protein 3

Paleo Refried Beans
Serves: 4
Prep Time: 15 Minutes

Ingredients

1 onion, peeled, diced
4 cloves garlic, peeled, minced
2 large eggplants
3 tbsp. tomato paste
1 tsp. cayenne pepper
1 tsp. oregano, cumin powder
1 tsp. black pepper
1 ½ tsp. salt, black pepper

Directions

Peel eggplant and slice into 1" cubes.

Heat 3 tbsp. coconut oil over medium heat, add onion, garlic, sauté for a minute.

Sauté in eggplant, cook for five minutes.

Add tomato paste, spices and salt, cover and continue to cook until eggplant is tender and released most of its juices.

Nutrition (g)
Calories 87
Fat 0
Sodium 599 (mg)
Carbs 20
Protein 3

Sweet Potato Nacho Chips
Serves: 6
Prep Time: 5 Minutes

Ingredients

2 sweet potatoes, peeled
3 tbsp. coconut oil
1 tsp. salt, black pepper

Directions

Preheat oven to 350 degrees and line two baking trays with parchment paper.

Slice potatoes as thinly as possible, toss with salt, black pepper, coconut oil.

Place slices on parchment paper without overlap and bake for 40 minutes, turn halfway through.

Nutrition (g)
Calories 176
Fat 10
Sodium 588 (mg)
Carbs 21
Protein 1

Guacamole
Serves: 4
Prep Time: 10 Minutes

Ingredients

2 avocados
1 clove garlic, peeled, crushed
2 tbsp. lime juice
1/2 red onion, peeled, minced
1 jalapeno, seeded, minced
Handful cilantro, chopped
1 tsp. cumin
1/2 tsp. salt

Directions

Place ingredients in blender and mix until fairly
smooth.

Nutrition (g)
Calories 220
Fat 20
Sodium 298 (mg)
Carbs 12
Protein 2

Beetroot Chips
Serves: 6
Prep Time: 5 Minutes

Ingredients

6 beetroots, peeled
3 tbsp. coconut oil
1/2 tsp. salt
1 tsp. coarse black pepper

Directions

Preheat oven to 375 degrees, line two baking sheets with parchment paper.

Slice beetroots into very thin slices, toss with salt and black pepper, and lay out on parchment paper.

Place in oven for 40 minutes, turn halfway through.

Nutrition (g)
Calories 155
Fat 11
Sodium 406 (mg)
Carbs 15
Protein 3

CONCLUSION

As you can see, these dishes are full of Mexican flavor but also very Paleo-friendly. To make the preparation a little easier, you can always prepare large batches of salsa which is always a great accompaniment for Mexican dishes. You can also prepare large batches of almond tortillas and freeze them in 2s and 4s for easy weeknight meals. Once you start preparing your Mexican favorites the Paleo way you will realize that clean substitutes to traditionally grain and fat-heavy dishes provide fresh, modern flavor and leave you feeling light and airy, now that is really great Mexican food!

Enjoy your month long Paleo-Mexican fiesta!